Wild Women
and
Tricky Ladies

Wild Women and Tricky Ladies

Rodeo Cowgirls, Trick Riders, and other Performing
Women Who Made the West Wilder

Jill Charlotte Stanford

TWODOT

Guilford, Connecticut
Helena, Montana
An imprint of Globe Pequot Press

A · TWODOT® · BOOK

To buy books in quantity for corporate use
or incentives, call **(800) 962–0973**
or e-mail **premiums@GlobePequot.com.**

TwoDot is an imprint of Globe Pequot Press and a registered trademark of Morris Book Publishing, LLC.
Text design and layout: Sheryl P. Kober
Project editor: John Burbidge

Library of Congress Cataloging-in-Publication Data
Stanford, Jill Charlotte.
  Wild women and tricky ladies : rodeo cowgirls, trick riders, and other
performing women who made the West wilder / Jill Charlotte Stanford.
       p. cm.
  Includes index.
  ISBN 978-0-7627-5870-8
  1. Women rodeo performers—West (U.S)—Biography. 2. Horsemen and
horsewomen—West (U.S.)—Biography. 3. Women rodeo performers—West
(U.S.)—History. 4. Horsemen and horsewomen—West (U.S.)—History. 5.
Trick riding—West (U.S.)—History. I. Title.
  GV1833.5.S73 2011
  791.8'40922—dc22
  [B]

                                        2010034510

Printed in the United States of America
10 9 8 7 6 5 4 3 2 1

To all those wild and wonderful early-day cowgirls who did it all—they rode the broncs, spun the ropes, did the tricks at a gallop, ran the relay races, and never forgot they were ladies. My admiration for them just grows and grows.

Texas rodeo female performers, 1920s. Standing from left: Florence Hughes Randolph, Ruth Roach, Mabel Strickland, Reine Hafley Shelton, Mildred Douglas, Bonnie McCarrol, Rose Smith, and Maud Tarr. Squatting from left: Bea Kirnan, Mayme Stroud, and Fox Hastings.

Contents

Contents

A Tip of the Stetson

First tip goes to Erin Turner, my wonderful editor. She encouraged me the whole way around the arena.

To Thomas Triplett, Esq., whose help and advice were more valuable to me than I can say.

To Jan Mendoza, who got the news and saddled up right away to help round up trick riders.

To Arlene LaMar, whose picture on the American Cowgirl Web site started this whole thing.

To Peggy Veach Robinson of Veach Saddlery in Trenton, Missouri. She opened up her files about trick saddles and made helpful suggestions all the way around the track. She also pointed out to me that "you twirl a baton, but you spin a rope," saving me some embarrassment.

To Karan Miller at *Western Horseman* magazine for finding a needle in a haystack.

To all my Cowgirls—Kate, Stormy, Marjorie, Bridget, Joan, and Nancy—who have been my greatest supporters!

To Coi Drummond-Gerhrig of the Denver Public Library photo sales, who once again took up the challenge and dug out wonderful images from the collections.

A cowgirl stands on her horse's saddle at the Calgary Exhibition and Stampede, Calgary, Alberta.

Glenbow Museum NA-3985-17

Introduction

This is how it all starts.

This little girl, Mary Ellen Petrasy Beal, always wanted a pony. At the fair one year, for one brief, shining moment, she was put on a patient photographer's pony, dressed in borrowed cowgirl clothing, and had her picture taken. She never forgot that moment.

What little girl who loves horses and riding hasn't tried standing up on her horse or pony like the beautiful trick riders she saw at the rodeo or fair? Or dreamed it in living color while snuggled in her bed—visions of flashy horses and breathtaking stunts being performed by *herself*.

Having a saddle to stand up on certainly helps, although the stunt can be done bareback and especially in bare feet. Carefully, cautiously, she rises up to a full standing position. Then, even though she is wavering a little and hoping her mount doesn't move, she stretches her arms out wide and smiles a big, Western cowgirl smile. She waves to the imaginary crowd before slipping back down into her saddle or her steed's bare back.

Mary Ellen Petrasy Beal smiling a cowgirl smile for the photographer.
Kate Aspen

At the Washington State Fair one year, I saw a beautiful woman who was not only standing up on a horse but was standing on three of them at once. Her two feet were on the outside horses. Then she jumped them over a barrier in the middle of the arena at a gallop. It goes without saying that she was smiling and waving.

Women trick riders have been a part of Wild West shows, rodeos, and fairs since the turn of the twentieth century and before. Bertha Blancett excelled at Roman riding at the Pendleton Round-Up, winning the race and the purse countless times. Tillie Baldwin's iconic picture "Fancy Riding"—of her doing a Hippodrome stand wearing bloomers—was taken in 1915 by Ralph Doubleday at the Pendleton Round-Up and hangs over my desk where I write, reminding me that I can do anything. After all, Tillie is standing on a galloping horse, arms out wide! That picture inspired me to write this book.

Other famous trick riders include Prairie Rose Henderson, Fox Hastings, Florence Hughes Randolph, and Lucille Mulhall. These women, and many others, trick rode and did fancy roping on horseback well into the late 1930s and 1940s.

During the 1940s through the 1960s, many women were trick riding. Most of them were self-taught. Ruth Davis taught herself and her horse at the same time. Arlene LaMar, a member of the

Cowgirl Rules

1. Shoot first.
2. Boots, hat, chaps—nothing else matters.
3. Drinking and shooting make a fine woman.
4. My rules are the only rules that count.
5. Never leave home without your rope.
6. The best friends are cowgirl friends.
7. If it don't make you smile, it ain't right.
8. If you're a good girl, you'll get a pony.*

*(There are only eight rules because cowgirls shouldn't have more rules than there are commandments.)

—Anji Gallanos,
a cowgirl from Juneau, Alaska

Flying Valkyries, appeared in countless shows as well as a movie starring Roy Rogers called *The Heart of the Rockies*.

Then, quite by chance, Madonna Eskew Pumphrey rode in. Her family history, along with her own feats of trick riding and roping, could be a book all by itself.

The Fender Drag, the Tail Drag, the Suicide Drag (sometimes called the Cossack or Russian Drag), the shoulder and side stands, and the big finish—the Hippodrome Stand—are still practiced today by modern-day trick riders.

Jan Mendoza lives in Northern California and teaches trick riding. She practices what she preaches too, appearing in rodeos and fairs all over the West.

Erin Mullis is one of our up-and-coming trick riders. With a BS in Agriculture in one hand and the reins of her flashy paint horse in the other, Erin is the embodiment of the modern-day trick rider.

Mary Rivers's stories of her exciting life as a trick rider as well as a circus performer are told here. Today she is teaching women of all ages, as well as their horses, the art of making the crowds catch their breath while the rider makes it look easy.

Carrying on the trick riders' tradition are the Riata Ranch Cowboy Girls. Located in Exeter, California, Riata Ranch International was created in 1957. This unique riding school for young people combines horsemanship and character development.

It is my great pleasure to share these stories and pictures of wild women and tricky ladies with you—all you girls who stood up on your horses or ponies, either for real or in your dreams.

Ride 'em cowgirl!
www.thatgirlproductions.com

Lucyle Richards signed this photo of her Roman riding to her friend Shirley Adams, whose father was George Adams, an early Wild West promoter. Shirley began her trick roping/riding career at the age of five.
Veach Saddlery Company, Trenton, Missouri

A SHORT GALLOP AROUND THE ARENA: TRICK RIDING EXPLAINED

Imagine that you are on a beautiful, flashy pinto horse galloping flat out. Now imagine standing up on that horse. You wave, arms extended and with both hands to the applauding and cheering crowd as you rocket past, the horse running free and, hopefully, straight ahead. When you get back down into the saddle, you throw your right leg over and around the tall pommel, slip your left leg into the strap attached to the saddle especially for this purpose, and then straighten your right leg up high. You grab your right foot with your right hand and raise your left arm into a salute. Don't forget to smile!

You have just completed the Hippodrome Stand and the Split to the Side. Next you will do the Cossack Drag and then pull yourself back up and into a One Foot Stand. As your big finish on your final run past the stands (which are just a blur to you), you have planned the Hippodrome again. You can hear the cheering, the whistles and the applause. You love it! The adrenaline is really pumping as you get back

> *That second clinched my inoculation with the spark of that nameless something that fires every trick rider's heart. A something that turns every defeat into a brand-new challenge.*
>
> **—Vera McGinnis, on placing second to Tillie Baldwin at the Winnipeg Stampede, 1913**

into the saddle and pull your horse up to a jog for a final pass to the appreciative crowd, waving and smiling as you exit.

Doesn't sound easy, does it? It's not. It is full of risk, danger—and thrills.

Trick riding originated with the Romans, who stood on their horses to race, sometimes on just one but often two or three at a time. This has evolved into our modern-day Roman riding stunt. The Greeks vaulted on horseback. As soon as they got horses, the Plains Indians quickly learned how to slip over their horse's back, shooting arrows or their rifles under the horse's neck while they were chasing buffalo. Russian Cossacks were master horsemen and used what we now call "trick riding" in battle as a form of psychological warfare to frighten the foot soldiers on the opposing side. The Cossack Drag is named for these peerless horsemen.

Many Cossacks left Russia and moved to America early in the 1800s. Speaking

I raced down the track and dropped into a *Russian Drag*—in which you put your right toe into a leather loop that is fastened into the cinching on the off side, then hang down on the left side of the horse, stick your left foot in the air, and trail your fingers in the dirt.

—Vera McGinnis, *Rodeo Road: My Life as a Pioneer Cowgirl*
(New York: Hastings House Publishers, 1974)

little or no English, they used their horsemanship to earn money by becoming entertainers. Audiences in the circus and other shows they rode in loved it, and trick riding became a Western favorite. It even became a rodeo event, with men and women attempting more and more daring feats and the hardest tricks earning the most points.

Trick and fancy roping was a big part of early-day Wild West shows as well as the ever-increasing rodeos throughout the West. At the famed Pendleton Round-Up in Pendleton, Oregon, the official Round-Up Souvenir Program for Wednesday, September 19, 1928, lists Trick and Fancy Roping beginning immediately following the "Spectacular Indian Parade." Trick Riding contestants are listed as Freddy Hunt, Reine Shelton, Donna Cowan, Buff Brady, Mable Strickland, and Vera McGinnis (who was famous for her under-the-belly crawl—beneath a horse running at full speed).

By 1946 the program lists Trick Riding as "Contracted." The riders are Monte Montana, Louise Montana, Betty Willis, Bob Rooker, Montie Montana Jr., Francis Stiller, and Emma "Pee Wee" Burge of Modesto, California.

World War II brought rodeo almost to a halt. When it returned, trick riding and roping was no longer a rodeo event earning points and prize money. It became a rodeo specialty act, strictly entertainment.

The good news is that more and more wild women are standing up, going over their horse's back, balancing on one foot, and learning the Suicide Drag, among other breathtaking stunts. Trick and fancy roping has never lost its appeal. The audience is still as enthusiastic today as it was when trick riding and roping first caught the spectators' attention.

A Saddle for Champions

Trick riders have known for ninety years where to go for the saddle that makes the tricks look easy.

Veach Saddlery Co., Inc., was founded in 1919 by Monroe Veach. Beginning in a modest way, Veach built a small twelve-by-eighteen-foot building and set to work

Mr. Monroe Veach
Trenton, Mo.

Dear Mr. Veach:

Under separate cover I am sending you the cruppers for the new trick riding saddle. I want a 15-inch tree, low cantle, sheepskin-covered fork and skirts with the initials T. J. R., silver horn, quilted seat, 1-inch-width string extra long but strong and pliable, D rings, and the extra rings on the cruppers so the flank can be set back farther if we want to tie down the back for different tricks.

Enclosed is a clipping with a splatter of ink where we want a ring on the saddle to fasten a breast collar. It must be a 1-inch ring and low.

We want the narrow oxbow stirrups and narrower fenders than the first saddle you made for me and reinforced stirrup leathers and the regular length under the belly straps.

I'm still using the first saddle you made for me, and every one admires it and asks who made it, and I always tell them a good saddle maker.

Please ship the saddle to T. J. Richard, Box 220, Greenwood, Miss., collect.

Thanking you for all past favors, I remain,

Yours truly
Lucyle Richards

making and repairing harnesses and saddles. His first saddle order was for a rural mail carrier, Orrin Wilson. Veach had worked as a cowhand for rancher P. A. Thompson. He learned to rope and ride and gained quite a bit of knowledge about saddles that were put to the real test of a cowboy's work.

Expanding the business, Veach started going to the rodeos. He not only got orders for saddles but also became a trick rider and roper himself, furthering his knowledge about what "real" cowboys and cowgirls needed. A 1939 catalog contains this quote from Monroe Veach: "There is no such thing as a rodeo without a Veach saddle . . . they just can't happen."

He also said, "Send in your order for any leather goods you may want. If we can't make it, forget it . . . It can't be made."

A testimony to Veach's popularity and satisfaction for his trick saddles is this letter written to him by Lucyle Roberts Richards.

Lucyle, once known as the "prettiest and best-dressed cowgirl," was a top headliner at rodeos all over the world during the 1930s. She specialized in saddle bronc riding but was a daring trick rider as well. Some interesting side notes about this skilled woman: Lucyle bought an airplane in 1939 and learned acrobatic flying. In 1941 she was arrested and charged with murdering her fourth husband. She claimed that she shot him in self-defense, and after deliberating for twenty-one hours, a jury found her not guilty. As a member of the Women Airforce Service Pilots, Lucyle made major contributions to the Allies by flying bombers between the U.S. and Britain.

The Veach logo has long stood for excellence.
Veach Saddlery Company, Trenton, Missouri

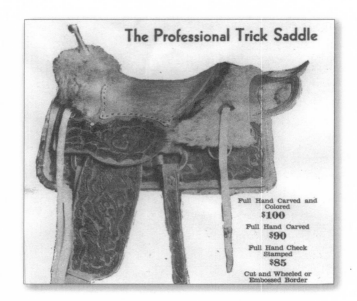

The letter was handwritten at the Hotel Ozarks, Springfield, Missouri, sometime during the 1930s. ("Every Room with Bath," "Smiling Service," and "Wonderful Foods in Our Coffee Shop.")The Veach family continues this legacy of making fine saddles for cowboys, cowgirls, and trick riders.

Gene Creed: Tricks and Broncs and Overalls

Born in 1904, Gene Creed grew up on a Colorado ranch, riding before she was five. Her first appearance at a rodeo was at the Watermelon Days Rodeo held at Rocky Ford, Colorado. She wore overalls. By 1925, and no longer in overalls, Gene was the youngest woman (age sixteen) to win the bronc riding at Cheyenne Frontier Days.

Gene competed in bronc and trick riding all over the United States, Mexico, and as far away as Australia. Inducted into the Cowgirl Hall of Fame at Hereford, Texas, in August 1982, she was given a trick-riding saddle made for her induction by Monroe Veach.

{ 2 }
THE GOLDEN AGE OF WILD WOMEN AND TRICKY LADIES

Following the Civil War, the West was settled and subdued for the most part. There were still occasional skirmishes between Indians and the settlers who were moving west, but on the whole it was all pretty tame by the turn of the twentieth century.

People still yearned for what they thought of as "the Real West"—a place where cowboys still rode magnificent horses, Indians war-whooped, and stagecoaches and pioneer wagons were in constant peril.

Before there were movies or television, a form of entertainment collectively known as the "Wild West Show" filled the void.

One of the first of these shows was L. O. Hillman's Wild West Aggregation (1900–1920), followed by Buckskin Bill's Wild West (1900). Stepping into the lucrative arena were Texas Jack's Wild West (1901–1905), Bud Atkinson's Circus and Wild West (early 1900s and an Australian tour in 1912), Jones Bros.' Buffalo Ranch Wild West (1910), Bronco Johns' Famous Western Horseman and his Corps of Expert Horsemen (1906), Buckskin Ben's Wild West and Dog and Pony Show (1908), Miller Bros. 101 Ranch Real Wild West (1907–1916,

> Women trick riders sustained many injuries from being dragged and stepped on, and a rider could end up just as dead from trick riding as she could from a bronc tromping.
>
> —Joyce Roach, *The Cowgirls*

Lillian Bergerhoff, a cowgirl in "The Red man Spectacle and Red Indian Camp," poses circa 1902 in front of a painted backdrop in the dirt arena at Empress Hall during the Golden West Exhibition at Earl's Court in London, England. She wears a cowboy hat, scarf, blouse, a corduroy split riding skirt, laced up boots, gauntlets with a star decoration (indicating she originates from Texas), a pistol with a leather holster and belt. She holds a lasso (lariat) in 1902.

Denver Public Library Z-2230

Della Ferrell, a native of Colorado and member of Buffalo Bill Cody's Wild West Show, poses on horseback in front of a painted backdrop at Earl's Court in England. Ferrell, a trick rider and roper, joined the show in 1887 as one of the "Western Girls." She wears a wide-brimmed hat with tassels hanging from its rim. Similar tassels hang around the edges of her short coat.

Denver Public Library NS-466

1925–1931), Kit Carson's Buffalo Ranch Wild West Show (1913), and the Irwin Brothers Cheyenne Frontier Days Wild West Show (1913–1917). And that's just the short list.

Perhaps the most famous of them all was Buffalo Bill's Wild West and Congress of Rough Riders—billed as "Americas Entertainment."

Buffalo Bill—in real life, former scout and bison hunter William F. Cody—knew just how to tap into what America wanted to see. He loved the West and tried to por-

Stastia Carry shows her stuff while competing in fancy riding in Toronto, Ontario, 1926.

Glenbow Archives
PA-3457-18

tray a vanishing and romanticized version to his eager audience. His high-end Wild West show consisted of a series of "historical events" featuring daring horsemanship, sharpshooting, and rodeo-style events. Buffalo Bill hired top cowhands and persuaded some Native Americans, notably Sitting Bull, to be a part of his show. Arabs, Mongols, and South American gauchos made up part of the thrilling entertainment.

Women were featured attractions in Buffalo Bill Cody's Wild West Show, and the spectators couldn't get enough of the sight of a woman doing the same gallant and daring things on horseback as the men.

For sixteen years Annie Oakley was one of the show's star attractions. Born Phoebe Ann Moses in 1886, Oakley first gained recognition as a sharpshooter at age fifteen by

Annie Oakley is watched closely by one of the Indians in the troupe—possibly Sitting Bull.

Bonnie Gray, on King Tut, not only jumped over an automobile full of Ellensburg Rodeo officials but was also Queen of the Rodeo in 1926. Her parents had high hopes for their daughter, who had a college degree in music and was a fine pianist. Bonnie, however, had other ideas!

Ellensburg (Washington) Public Library RDO-053

defeating professional marksman Frank Butler in a shooting exhibition. (She married him a few years later, and he became her manager.)

Annie was billed in the show as "Miss Annie Oakley, the Peerless Lady Wing-Shot." Sitting Bull, a Sioux warrior who participated in the Battle of the Little Bighorn and was another of the show's featured attractions, called her "Little Sure Shot."

Annie was quite the marksman. From thirty paces she was able to split the edge of a playing card, hit the ace of spades dead center, shoot down a playing card tossed in the air, shatter glass balls thrown into the air, hit dimes held between Butler's fingers, shoot an apple out of a poodle's mouth, and shoot off the glowing end of a cigarette

Wearing formal dress,
two jumpers sail over a
car in perfect tandem.

Veach Saddlery Company,
Trenton, Missouri

from Butler's mouth, proving his faith in her "eye." She even shot a cigarette out of Crown Prince Wilhelm's hand when the troupe traveled to Berlin.

Her most famous trick involved a mirror. Annie could hit a target behind her, shooting backwards over her shoulder while holding a mirror up for aim.

Another wild woman and rival to Annie Oakley for a time was Lillian Smith. When Lillian was seven years old, she asked her father for a "small rifle." She took

A Charlie Russell cowgirl.

Author's collection

to shooting right away and it wasn't long before her father, also her manager, was offering a $5,000 reward to anyone who could outshoot the ten-year-old. Doc Carver, one of the best-known marksmen of the time, took the challenge but never showed up at the competition held in St. Louis.

During a tour in California in 1886, Buffalo Bill brought Smith into the show for the summer, billing the fifteen-year-old as the "Champion California huntress." Annie Oakley eventually prevailed, but at a price: She took six years off her real age to compete with the younger shooter.

Calamity Jane, who was born in 1852 as Martha Jane Cannary, was another participant in Wild Bill's show. Calamity Jane was a notorious frontierswoman who was the subject of many wild stories—many of which she made up herself. In the show she was a skilled horsewoman and expert rifle and revolver handler.

Ethyle and Juanita Perry were beautiful and talented twins. Billed as "The Cossack Girls," they performed the difficult moves made by Russian Cossack cavalrymen. When not doing death-defying drags, they rode wild horses to a standstill and threw their ropes at assorted bulls and calves, always with success.

Wild Women and Tricky Ladies

"Daughter of the West" postcard.

Author's collection

This vintage postcard shows a cowgirl ready for the rodeo. Author's collection

I went to this today. They sure had some pretty trick riders. I am going back tomorrow.

—Written on the back of a postcard depicting the Pendleton Round-Up, 1924

Everybody wanted to be a cowgirl! May Peterson, a soprano with the Metropolitan Opera, doffs her hat and rides the old gray mare at the St. Paul National Legion Convention, 1912.

Author's collection

MAY PETERSON
SOPRANO—METROPOLITAN OPERA FAME
THE PRIMA DONNA WHO RODE THE OLD GRAY MARE AT ST. PAUL NATIONAL LEGION CONVENTION.

Concert Bookings: Write Haensel & Jones, Aeolian Hall, New York.

Women in early-day rodeos and Wild West shows competed in everything from saddle bronc riding to bull-dogging and trick riding and roping. The audience especially loved specialty races, such as relay and Roman races. With the advent of the motorcar, women took to jumping their horses over a car parked in the middle of the arena.

The Wild West shows never left the stage completely, even though movies were becoming popular. Bee Ho Gray's Wild West (circa 1919–1932), Barrett Shows and Oklahoma Bill's Wild West (1920), Gene Autry's Flying A Ranch Stampede (1942), and the Austin Bros. 3 Ring Circus and Real Wild West (1945) kept the stands packed with thrilling action featuring everything from shoot-'em-ups to Indians on the warpath to pretty cowgirls spinning ropes and doing their fancy trick riding.

A Roman rider leaps over a convertible.
Veach Saddlery Company, Trenton, Missouri

Rodeos were springing up all over the western United States and Canada. One of them was Col. Jim Eskew's JE Rodeo, started in 1930. Colonel Eskew is credited with bridging the gap between Wild West shows and the modern rodeo.

The women galloped on over to the rodeos in both the United States and Canada, and they made good money for their efforts. A top performer, competing in a top rodeo, could clear $1,000 in a single event.

Trick riding and roping was not without its dangers, and many women were hurt—some seriously, some escaping with just a bruise, a cut, or a case of wounded pride. Ruby Roberts, who began trick riding in 1925, broke both ankles, one arm, and two ribs in an accident. She healed and went right back to trick riding. Vera McGinnis fell from her horse in a 1934 relay race, suffering a broken neck and hip, a collapsed lung, and four fractured vertebrae.

Cowgirl bronc riding was outlawed in many rodeos after Bonnie McCarroll, an extremely popular cowgirl, couldn't free herself from the stirrups and was tragically trampled to death during a ride in 1929.

The trick riders and ropers continued to invent new and daring athletic moves on top of, and sometimes under, their galloping horses. They also perfected handling their ropes with ease.

The early days of rodeo—from 1910 to the mid 1920s—has been dubbed "The Golden Age." Before they had the vote, intrepid women were competing in rodeos against the cowboys, performing in Wild West shows, and generally shocking—as well as delighting—the crowds with their horsemanship, showmanship, pluck, and daring.

The list of the early-day "tricky ladies" is long, but several are standouts. Their stories are tales of courage against a world that felt women should stay in the kitchen, not show even an ankle, and behave themselves!

Trick and Fancy Roping Explained

Trick roping involves catching running animals by throwing a loop at them. There can be as many as ten animals, usually horses with riders on top and going through the loop with the roper standing at the side. This is a breathtaking show of skill and never fails to draw applause. In another stunt, catching all four legs of the animal earned extra points.

Fancy roping is spinning the rope at various speeds to create shapes and different positions. In competition, it was (and still is) a requirement that the ropers must demonstrate their skill both on foot and on horseback.

Trick and fancy roping for both cowgirls and cowboys is still a popular entertainment at rodeos today, although not as many women rope.

Peggy Minor made her trick-riding debut during the WW II Posse Horse Shows that were held in Ellensburg, Washington, when rodeos were banned by national defense officials. In 1947 Peggy bought a trick horse from Monty Montana, one of the best ropers to ever spin a rope. This photo, taken in 1948, shows Peggy spinning four ropes at once.

Ellensburg (Washington) Public Library RDO-066

Prairie Rose Henderson: Fearless and Flashy

One of the best loved of the old-time cowgirls was Prairie Rose Henderson. Known for her daring and skill on top of pitching broncos, this flamboyant cowgirl also rode in relay races and was a talented trick rider. She was well liked by the other women competitors.

What really set her apart—aside from her fearlessness and grit—were the outfits that she designed and sewed herself, combining sequins, fur, ostrich feathers, and any other trim she could rustle up. Her outfits were considered very daring, showing quite a bit of leg beneath the bloomers she preferred wearing over the full-legged divided skirts the other cowgirls wore. She outfitted her horses in silver.

Born Ann Robbins in Bristol, Ohio, somewhere during the early 1880s (she never revealed her exact age), she left Bristol in her dust at an early age and headed west. She took the name Prairie Rose for the flower that bloomed on the Wyoming prairies and Henderson from her first—but not her last—husband.

Prairie Rose invented herself as a rodeo performer. According to some accounts, as early as 1901 she asked to ride in the bucking horse event at the Cheyenne, Wyoming, Frontier Days Rodeo. When she was told that the "bylaws" allowed only men, she firmly demanded to see those bylaws. Of course there were none. She rode. If that story is true, she was the first woman to ride a bucking horse, for money, at a rodeo.

She hit the circuit and went to as many rodeos as she could find. By 1910 she was queen at the Pendleton Round-Up. In 1911 she was awarded

I regard myself as a woman who has seen much of life.

—Belle Starr, as stated to the *Fort Smith Elevator* about a year prior to her death

Prairie Rose Henderson mounted on a flashy pinto horse for a grand entry.

> *How can I explain to dainty, delicate women what it's like to climb down into a rodeo chute onto the back of a wild horse?*
>
> **—Fanny Sperry Steele, bronc rider**

the title of champion and started riding for the Irwin Brothers Wild West Show, wowing the crowds, who had never seen a woman as flamboyant and spunky as Prairie Rose.

In 1917 she won the coveted Union Pacific Railroad silver belt buckle after winning the bronc-riding contest at Cheyenne, Wyoming. She continued to compete at rodeos all over the west and went to Canada several times.

Prairie Rose left the circuit in 1932 and went to live with her last husband, Charles Coleman (who just happened to be a cattle rustler), at the Hadsell Ranch near the Green Mountains northwest of Rawlins, Wyoming. He was arrested soon after, but Prairie Rose stayed at the ranch.

Coleman got out of jail a few weeks later, but Prairie Rose was not at the ranch upon his return. It was mystifying, but Coleman probably thought that she had just got an itchy foot and "upped and left."

On July 17, 1939, a Mexican sheepherder who was fighting a brush fire in the area found Prairie Rose's body in a box canyon, a halter still clutched in her skeletal hand and her grain bucket nearby. She was identified by her ring and articles of clothing, including her cherished silver buckle. She had been trying to catch a horse and had frozen to death in a snowstorm.

Prairie Rose Henderson and Valentine.

The Pendleton Cowgirl Company

Tillie Baldwin: Bravado in Bloomers

Born in Avendale, Norway, in 1888, this cowgirl started life as Anna Matilda Wagner. Trained at an early age as a hairdresser, she never cut her own blond hair, which reached to her waist, almost always in a neat braid. An all-around athlete when she emigrated to America at the age of fourteen, she could not speak English but quickly learned and made friends.

Working as a hairdresser on Staten Island, she was inspired by a cowgirl movie being filmed that featured trick riding. Despite that fact that she did not know how to ride a horse and had never been west of New York, Anna was determined to learn trick riding. One can only imagine how tough this was for her, but learn she did!

Good enough to join Captain Jack Baldwin's Wild West Show in 1911, where she changed her name to Tillie Baldwin. Did she have a relationship with Captain Jack, or did she simply like the name? No one knows.

Tillie left Captain Jack and joined Will Rogers's vaudeville troupe and then moved on to the more prestigious 101 Ranch Show in 1912 with top billing. She rode in her first real rodeo in 1911 in Los Angeles, California, where she won the bronc riding. In 1912 she won both the trick riding and bronc riding contests at the Pendleton Round-Up in Pendleton, Oregon.

It was about at this time that Tillie adopted the gymnast's bloomer outfit, which was safer than the divided skirts most women wore and also made her stand out in a competitive field. She wound her neat braid up behind her head, and the crowds went wild over this new look for trick riders.

She with the most certainty wins.

—Nancy Becker,
cowgirl and glass artist

TILLIE BALDWIN
WOMAN WORLDS CHAMPION BUCKING HORSE
TRICK "N" FANCY RIDER
ONLY WOMAN BULL DOGGER

4
COPYRIGHT 1913
R.H. PRICE

Tillie Baldwin chose to wear a gymnast's outfit for her trick riding.

ROMAN RACE, RIDERS JOHNNIE MULLENS, TILLIE BALDWIN + A.J. BRYSON, WINNIPEG STAMPEDE 1913,

Tillie Baldwin stays out in front in the Roman Race at the Winnipeg Stampede, Manitoba, 1913.
Glenbow Archives NA-1029-18

Bitten by the rodeo bug, she started her professional career in 1913 at the Winnipeg Stampede in Canada and excelled at all events. This fearless and athletic cowgirl moved it up a notch by entering the Roman Race—standing on the backs of two galloping horses. She collapsed following the race, but despite doctors' orders to rest, she was back on top of the horses the very next day—and defeated an otherwise all-male field. Tillie was so athletic that she would vault from one horse to the back of another in full stride for another lap around the arena, which she generally won. She went on to try bulldogging—wrestling full-grown steers to the ground—an event most women wouldn't even try.

Wild Women and Tricky Ladies

WORLDS CHAMPION LADY
BRONCHO BUSTER & TRICK RIDER
MISS TILLIE BALDWIN, Nº 4012
STAMPEDE CALGARY 1919

Tillie Baldwin sits on a stationary horse for a change. Calgary Stampede, Alberta, 1919.

FANCY ROPING BY TILLIE BALDWIN & HORACE DAY.　"STAMPEDE" WINNIPEG 1913.

Tillie Baldwin and a young Horace Day fancy roping at the Winnipeg Stampede, Manitoba, 1913.

Glenbow Archives NA-1029-21

Tillie, now a big star, went home to Norway for a visit in 1919, where she thrilled the crowds who came to see "one of their own" demonstrate what cowgirls in the United States were doing. Returning to the United States, she continued to ride the rodeo circuit and was billed as the "Woman World Champion Bucking Horse, Trick and Fancy Rider."

Tillie married William Slate in 1925 and started to slow down—just a little bit. The couple moved to Connecticut, but Tillie was not done with horses, not just yet. She taught riding and vaulting on horseback at a nearby riding academy, and every once in a while she would perform in a Wild West show. She died in 1958.

In 2004 the Madam Alexander Doll Company made a limited-edition Tillie Baldwin doll to commemorate this beautiful and fearless rider.

Bertha Kaepernik Blancett: Champion Lady Rider of the World

Bertha Kaepernik Blancett was involved with the world of horses and rodeo from the beginning. At a very early age her father put her up on top of a horse and said, "Now, Bertha, stay on!" And stay on she did—for her entire life.

She was a strong girl who just loved turning unbroken horses on her family's ranch near Sterling, Colorado, into good saddle horses. In 1904, while just a teenager, Bertha rode a bucking horse (her own—it was not unusual to own your own bucking horse) as an exhibition during Cheyenne Frontier Days. A rain shower had made the arena muddy, and the men refused to compete. Bertha scoffed at the rain and mud and put on an exhibition that brought the crowds to their feet.

> When I first started to ride, we wore divided skirts and tied them below the knees when we did fancy riding, being very careful not to expose any leg between the skirt and the boot top.
>
> —Vera McGinnis

**Bertha Blancett,
Champion Lady Rider
of the World, Round-Up,
1914.**

For many of them, it was the first time they had ever seen a "lady" astride a horse.

She won her first rodeo title in 1905 and was soon making a name for herself as a bronc rider, adding some trick riding and the popular relay races to her repertoire. Relay races featured cowgirls racing three times around a track, changing horses after each circuit. Bertha took lots of chances in relay riding, crouching far over her horse's neck and leaning into the turns. Her ability to change horses without ever touching the ground made her a sure bet for the spectators.

Bertha joined several Wild West shows, including the 101 Ranch Show, where she met and married bulldogger Del Blancett. She often worked as his hazer. In steer wrestling, a hazer is a cowhand who rides alongside the steer to keep it running in a straight line. This makes the steer wrestler's job easier when jumping from her horse.

Bertha Blancett won the ladies relay race at the Calgary Exhibition and Stampede, Alberta, 1912.

Glenbow Museum NA-335-18

Bertha and Dell moved to California, lured by the newfangled moving pictures being shot there. A popular subject was the Wild West, and she and Del fit right in. Under contract to Bison Pictures, she met and worked with Tom Mix, Bebe Daniels, and Hoot Gibson.

In 1911 Bertha heard about the Pendleton Round-Up and traveled north to Oregon. What a performance she put on to the estimated crowd of twelve thousand! Bronc riding, of course. She trick rode as well, flying past the packed and cheering stands in her own version of the Hippodrome Stand. Along with the "purse," the prize for winning included a pair of fringed and beaded gauntlets—leather gloves with an extended cuff, which are now on display, along with her leather skirt, trophies, and various other items from her rodeo life at the Pendleton Round-Up Hall of Fame.

Bertha was an all-around cowgirl at the Pendleton Round-Up from 1911 to 1918, where she successfully competed with the best riders of her era, both men and women. As a bronc rider, Bertha set herself apart from most other cowgirls by riding "slick," never hobbling her stirrups under the horse's belly.

Bertha Blancett performed in Wild West shows in the United States and Australia and competed in many rodeos.

She was very popular at the Calgary Stampede in 1913, entering and winning the relay race, trick riding, and roping competitions as well as bronc riding.

In 1914 Bertha came within twelve points of winning the all-around title. As far as the cowboys were concerned, it was too close for comfort—the rules were changed, separating women into their own category.

World War I brought rodeo nearly to a stop. To help fill the gaps and keep people buying tickets, Bertha took up fancy roping as well as Roman Racing—standing on two horses, a foot on each, as they tore around the track. Many people could not believe it was a woman out there thundering flat out by the stands.

Killed in action, Del never came back from the Great War. During the 1919 Pendleton Round-Up, Bertha wore a black armband with a gold star on it on her right arm. She never remarried.

In 1922, at the age of thirty-nine, Bertha took a job as a guide in Yellowstone National Park and packed horses and mules, as well as "dudes," into the wilderness for nine years.

A cowwoman takes no coddling, gets no martyr complex just because she is going to have a baby.

—**Alice Greenough, World Champion Bronc Rider, 1933 and 1941**

In 1961 the Pendleton Round-Up Association honored her as grand marshal of the Westward Ho! Parade.

During her sixties, when most women her age were sitting and knitting, Bertha was working in rodeos as a pickup rider. The cowboys who drew Bertha to get them off the pitching horses after their ride were happy for her expertise and knowledge of how a "bucker" acts.

Bertha eventually retired to Andy Jauregui's J Spear Ranch in Pomona, California. She died in 1981.

Fox Hastings: Always Smiling for the Cheering Crowd

Wearing possibly the most uniquely shaped Stetson hat on top of her red hair, Fox Hastings made a name for herself by becoming one of the first and only female bull-doggers in rodeo history. In addition to wrestling steers to the ground, she was a trick rider too.

This flamboyant cowgirl was born Eloise Fox. She ran away from her California home and convent school when she was four-teen and started her rise in rodeo on bucking horses and with trick riding. While a member of the Irwin Brother's Wild West Show, she did her stunts on one of the fastest trick riding horses performing at that time.

> To the rodeo crowd she is Fox Hastings, cowgirl extraordinary. To neighbors, she is Mrs. Mike Hastings, a good cook and tidy housekeeper.
>
> —Newspaper article

She's lost her hat and the wind has mussed her hair, but *Fox Hastings* has successfully bulldogged a steer at the Ellensburg Roundup, 1928.

Ellensburg (Washington) Public Library RDO-012

FOX HASTING BULLDOGGING ELLENSBURG RODEO 1928 (DOUBLEDAY)

Marrying Mike Hastings, a fellow rodeo star and renowned bulldogger, she dropped her first name and became Fox Hastings. With her husband's help and guidance, she made her bulldogging debut at a 1924 rodeo in Houston, Texas. Her fastest time was seventeen seconds, setting a record not only for the cowboys but also as the only woman to compete in what was thought of as a man's sport.

Fox had a terrific sense of style. She loved bold colors and wore enormous bows in her red hair when she wasn't wearing her signature hat. When she was bulldogging, she wore what the cowboy steer wrestlers wore—tall boots laced to the knees, knickers, turtleneck sweaters, and a leather football helmet. She would say, before rocketing

Wearing her signature Stetson, jodphurs, and tall boots, Fox Hastings waits behind the chutes for her next event.

Cowgirls, Rodeo, Cheyenne, Wyo.

I can do it because I can do anything. —Sonora Carver

out of the chute after a steer, "If I can just get my fanny out of the saddle and my feet planted, there's not a steer that can last against me." Nothing fazed her. She would come up smiling at the camera while lying in the mud, still clinging to the neck of a recently thrown steer.

Fox's career was marked by injuries and spectacular peformances, as this account illustrates:

> *Notable among the special attractions was Fox Hastings,*
> *who, though she had suffered a broken rib the day before the show opened,*
> *bulldogged her steer each of the three days of the rodeo proper. She had a contract*
> *to fulfill and she couldn't let the management down.*

The stresses of being on the road traveling to rodeo performances put a great deal of stress on the marriage, which ended in divorce. The marriage might have ended, but Fox kept the Hastings name.

During the 1940s, Fox developed tuberculosis. She had remarried, and her husband, Chuck Wilson, was by her side through several agonizing years of treatment. Fox recovered and was in remission when another blow struck her. On August 2, 1948, Chuck Wilson died of a heart attack. Two weeks later, at the Adams Hotel in Phoenix, Arizona, the fifty-year-old cowgirl died of self-inflicted gunshot wounds to the head and stomach. She left the following note to her employer: "I didn't want to live without my husband."

Left: All the trick riders were close friends, as this photo shows. Can you spot Fox's hat and Prairie Rose's flamboyant outfit?

Author's collection

If you are riding a high horse, there is no way to get off it gracefully.

—Calamity Jane

Florence Hughes Randolph takes the inside track against her male competitors while Roman Racing at the Pendleton Round-Up, circa 1918.

Madonna Eskew Pumphrey

Florence Hughes Randolph: A Cowgirl Who Did It All!

Standing only four feet, six inches tall and weighing just ninety pounds, Florence Hughes was nevertheless a giant in the annals of women in rodeo. She made more than 500 rodeo appearances and was a fierce competitor in trick roping, trick and Roman riding, and saddle bronc. She was World Champion Cowgirl Trick Rider ten times and was awarded the trophy for World Champion Bronc Rider.

Rodeo was not her only arena. Early in her career, the Wild West shows headlined her and she formed her own Princess Mohawk's Wild West Hippodrome.

Florence Hughes Randolph did it all, including riding bucking horses.
Madonna Eskew Pumphrey

She was born Cleo Alberta Holmes in August, Georgia, in 1898, but her father started calling her Florence, and the name stuck. Florence did not begin riding horses until she was thirteen, although she rode mules bareback around her father's plantation.

Florence must have been a persuasive young woman, because she convinced her parents to allow her to apprentice with a trick riding circus family. By the time she was fourteen years old, she was riding with Col. King's IXL Ranch Wild West Show. She stayed until she was sixteen.

Always a crowd favorite, the Hippodrome Stand almost looked easy when Florence Hughes Randolph did it.

Madonna Eskew Pumphrey

FLORENCE RANDOLPH LADY CHAMPION TRICK RIDER. (DOUBLEDAY)

Imagine hanging from the straps and still smiling! That's what Florence Hughes Randolph is doing in this Side Drag.

Her specialties were trick and Roman riding. In 1919 she shot to stardom by outriding fourteen men in a Roman Race competition. She had learned to spin a rope by then as well. She was completely fearless—the only woman to turn a backward somersault from the back of one horse to another. In fact, she was the only woman to even try.

Her feats were not without peril, however. She once said she had "been carried

Arena ballerina stays in step with her steed.
The Pendleton Cowgirl Company

off for dead several times." A few years later, after another fall, she awoke in the hospital only to overhear a doctor say that if she lived, she might never walk again. Wrapped only in a sheet, Florence bolted out of bed and left the building.

Florence married cowboy Floyd Randolph in 1925 and was billed as Florence Hughes Randolph after that. She always credited her husband for the new and daring tricks she perfected.

She worked in the newly emerging movie industry, doubling for movie stars. She even became one of Mack Sennett's bathing beauties! In 1927 Metro-Goldwyn-Mayer Studios awarded Florence the $100,000 silver "Champion Cowgirls" trophy in Madison Square Garden.

Not content to retire from the rodeo world she loved, Florence produced and managed the Ardmore Rodeo in Ardmore, Oklahoma, where her granddaughter Madonna Eskew Pumphrey, herself a talented rodeo trick rider and roper, lives today.

Tad Lucas and Mitzi Lucas Riley: A Mother-Daughter Team

Championship rodeo trick rider Mitzi Lucas Riley appeared in a "comic strip–style" ad for Camel cigarettes. Titled "Hairbreadth Escape," the drawings show Mitzi doing the Back Drag. In the next frame, Mitzi's horse shies and the crowd gasps in horror. Mitzi is being pulled under her horse! The next thrilling picture shows Mitzi pulling herself up while the crowd yells, "She's all right now—she'll pull herself up!" In the last frame, Mitzi is in the stall (with her horse), enjoying a cigarette! This was not uncommon for the time—many athletes endorsed tobacco products.

Mitzi was born to Buck (a bulldogger and bronc rider) and Tad (a famous trick rider and rodeo star) Lucas. Tad was a free spirit who joined a Wild West show at an early age. Her first performance was in England. Tad and Mitzi formed a trick-riding

Tad Lucas
National Cowgirl Museum and Hall of Fame

Mitzi Lucas Riley
National Cowgirl Museum and Hall of Fame

team when Mitzi was just six years old. They performed together for twenty years, and Tad made all their costumes.

The mother-daughter relationship continued with their induction into the National Cowgirl Museum and Hall of Fame—Tad in 1978 and Mitzi in 1996.

Florence La Due: Champion Lady Fancy Roper of the World

Trick and fancy roper Florence La Due, who was also known as Flores, is still considered one of the very best ever to spin a rope.

Florence La Due performs a fancy rope trick at the Calgary Stampede, 1912.

Glenbow Archives NA-628-4

Born in Minnesota in 1883, she grew up on a Sioux Indian reservation, where her her grandfather was the Indian agent. She joined the Cummins Wild West and Indian Congress show in 1905 and met and married her husband, fancy roper Guy Weadick, in 1906.

At the Calgary Stampede in 1912, her greatest rival for the trick and fancy roping contest was Lucille Mulhall. Florence was able to tie a double hitch in a slack rope with just two quick wrist movements. She won the contest, the first of three world championships.

A group of cowgirls at the Calgary Exhibition and Stampede, Alberta, September 1912.
Glenbow Archives NA-3985-4

Florence La Due poses with her husband, Guy Weadick, founder of the Calgary Exhibition and Stampede.

Glenbow Archives NA-3164-70

{ 3 }
TALES FROM THE ARENA

Rodeo had to struggle to make a comeback after World War II. Because of security, many of the major rodeos had been canceled for the duration of the war. But America needed something to feel good about after the devastating war on two fronts, and the all-American sport of rodeo filled the bill for the avid fans of the "Old West."

The rodeo was the place where a pretty cowgirl galloped around the arena carrying the American flag, stirring patriotic hearts. The rodeo events of bronc busting, saddle bronc riding, wild bull riding, steer wrestling, calf roping, and team roping were fast and furious and brought the ever-increasing crowds to their feet.

How Cowgirls Got Their Name

The term "cowgirl" can be attributed to Lucille Mulhall.

Known as "America's Greatest Horsewoman and Queen of the Range," Lucille was to appear at Madison Square Garden in 1905. Newspapers of the day had been trying to describe this female phenomenon of the rodeo world. Some of the terms they came up with were "Female Conqueror of Beef and Horn" and "Lassoer in Lingerie." Others took a simpler route, calling her a "Cowboy Girl" and "Ranch Queen."

Eventually they invented a word that aptly described the lifestyle and talents of a woman who could rope and ride and do ranch work alongside men. That word was "cowgirl."

Lucille Mulhall performs at the San Antonio Rodeo circa 1925–1926.

Erwin E. Smith Foundation, Erwin E. Smith Collection, Library of Congress, on Deposit at the Amon Carter Museum, Fort Worth, Texas LC.S6.933

An accomplished rider early in her life, Dorothy Looney became one of the best female trick riders in the northwest. Seattle is a long ways from Ellensburg, but many fans from the big city often attended the rodeo just to watch her!

Ellensburg (Washington) Public Library RDO-009

No longer competitions that offered prize money, trick riding and trick roping were gaining in popularity as entertainment. For every trick rider who swept past the grandstands, there were several pairs of young eyes watching her every move. Young women were attracted to the daring stunts, and many of them went home to practice on horses that must have thought they had lost their minds as their riders suddenly stood up on their saddles or even their bare backs.

She sure ain't much to look at, but she sure as hell can ride.

—A remark about Calamity Jane, overheard at a performance of Buffalo Bill Cody's Wild West Show

Through courage and grit, many of them succeeded, becoming full-fledged trick riders and trick ropers. Some of them were lucky enough to have the older trick riders and ropers instruct them. Many of them taught themselves (and their horses) the tricks, sewed their own outfits, and joined the rodeo circuit, carrying on the tradition.

Arlene LaMar: From Kansas to Hollywood

Put together bright red hair, red-and-white Tony Lama boots, and a sporty red car and you've got Arlene LaMar, whose nickname, not surprisingly, is "Red." No bigger than a minute but packed with an hour's worth of spunk, this girl from Kansas went out and did it her way.

"My life began on a small farm around Kingsdown, Ford County, Kansas, but I won't say exactly when," Arlene says. "I was the youngest of eleven children, and I started riding when I was five years old."

If it had four legs, Arlene—as well as her sister, Cretia—was on it. A bull calf made a fine mount for a while. Later a horse named Babe helped Arlene become a trick rider.

"I dropped out of school before the eighth grade and helped on the farm with the chores," she recalls.

She was taken to her first rodeo and was dazzled by the trick riders. A quick learner, she would go home and make the straps that she had seen on the riders' saddles. On Babe she practiced the tricks she had seen. All alone out in a back pasture, with a barbed-wire fence to keep Babe going straight, Arlene (barefoot) was up in the Hippodrome Stand, off on the Fender Drag, and generally throwing herself all over Babe's neck, rump, and back.

"I was always a daredevil," she laughs. "I kept going to the rodeos, and I kept practicing. I even got myself a trick saddle. I bought *Western Horseman* magazine often. In one issue I responded to an ad from Mr. and Mrs. Joe Stoddard of Napa, California, asking for girl riders. I sent them a letter, and in return they wanted me to join them. I left home and went to their small ranch."

Roman Rider Arlene LaMar and her five white performing horses.

Arlene LaMar

Ernie Kirkpatrick of Bradford, Pennsylvania, who had ridden with the White Horse Ranch Troupe, taught Arlene Roman riding. Later Donna Rosium of South Dakota, who had also ridden for the White Horse Ranch, joined the Stoddards and became Arlene's close friend.

"We trained for three months before going on the road. Our first show was a fair at Jordan Valley, Oregon, then on to Winnemucca, Nevada, showing at their fair. I was on the racetrack doing my One Foot Stand in the saddle when a piece of paper blew in front of my horse, Silver. She shied and I landed on the track. They helped me off the track; I walked around a little and went back riding."

After Winnemucca they were on the road again. Arlene continues, "Donna and I drove the Stoddards' car behind them in the truck with the horses. At one point we were going so slow up a mountain that I left our car and jumped on the running board of the front truck to ask a question. Mrs. Stoddard didn't expect me and got so scared that she told me not to do that anymore!

HELP WANTED

WANTED: Two girl riders, ages 12 to 20 yrs. Experienced or will train. Wages and schooling. Write Mrs. Joe Stoddard, 1037 Fourth Ave., Napa, Calif.

This *Western Horseman* ad from September 1949 caught the attention of Arlene LaMar.

Printed with permission of *Western Horseman*

When we showed at the Napa, California, Mental Hospital, some of the patients climbed the fence and scared the horses so much that we thought we would need to leave the horses at the hospital. Then we went to the Veterans Administration Hospital and finally on to the Stockton State Fair and Rodeo.

At the rodeo Arlene met movie star Bill Elliot, who played Wild Bill Hickok and other Western heroes in the movies. Elliot was the grand marshal of the rodeo.

"After we did our riding, we were on the racetrack with our horses. Bill Elliot had his horse, Stormy Night, tied to the railing. I mentioned to Donna that I was going to ask Bill if I could ride Stormy Night. I went over and asked him and he said, 'Sure.' He gave me a leg up, as the stirrups were too long—he was six four! During that process

As one of the Flying Valkyries, Arlene LaMar stands on the back of Trigger (the "Wonder Horse") with Roy Rogers.

Arlene LaMar

An exuberant Arlene LaMar does not seem to mind that she is upside down at a gallop—just look at her smile!
Arlene LaMar

he about threw me on the other side of Stormy Night!"

In San Francisco the girls and their white horses rode in the Fourth of July parade down Market Street to City Hall. "We rode bareback," Arlene explains. "My horse, Frosty, jumped every white line at the intersections. That was exciting, and the people on the street clapped! They thought it was a stunt, so I just waved back at them like it was."

After San Francisco, they went on to Palm Springs, California, where they rode in the Desert Circus Parade, finally wintering at the Lazy C Ranch in Palm Springs. They didn't rest for long.

Four horsepower takes on a new meaning as Arlene LaMar jumps the hurdle standing on their backs.

Arlene LaMar

"We had a show at 1000 Oaks in the Mojave Desert," Arlene says. "The Stoddards had a beautiful albino stallion that I rode bareback and jumped a five-foot hurdle with. When I rode into the jump, I put the reins under my leg and threw my hands in the air as we went over the jump. I needed to get the reins back in my hands as soon as we hit the other side. He liked to buck after a jump."

While the Stoddards and their show were at the Banning, California, fairgrounds, they met Frank and Lois Hall, who had a son and daughter. The daughter wanted to learn how to Roman ride, and the Stoddards wanted to sell out, so the Halls bought the show.

The new show was named The Valkyries and Their Flying White Horses. The Valkyries moved to the Broken Arrow Ranch on Sherman Drive in North Hollywood and started doing benefits and live TV shows. The ranch had a nice arena, and every Sunday they had practice and jackpot roping with quite a few PRCs (Professional Rodeo Cowboys) attending.

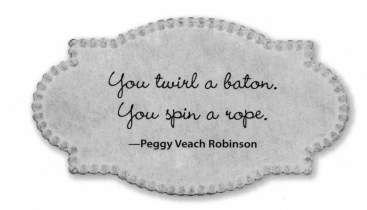

You twirl a baton. You spin a rope.

—Peggy Veach Robinson

Their new trainer was Merle Christenson, who was a double for Roy Rogers. The Valkyries were chosen to be in a movie at Republic Studios, *The Heart of the Rockies*.

Arlene says, "We were on the set four days for our part in the movie. We did a square dance on our white horses, with Roy calling the dance. Donna and I had to ride under a gate and stop, turn our heads toward the camera, and smile. Donna jumps the five horses in the movie."

During a publicity photo shoot with famous cinematographer Sid Hickock, the girls and their horses posed for several photos with Roy and his palomino, Trigger. They did a photo of all the Valkyries standing on their white horses with Roy, and then Hickock said, "How 'bout you sit on Trigger, Roy, and one of the girls can stand behind you, with the other six horses three on each side?" Roy agreed and said to Arlene "You'll do." She hopped onto Trigger's broad back behind Roy and remembers that Mr. Rogers was "a real nice guy." The movie was released in 1951 and is still considered a Western classic.

In 1950 at the Los Angeles Coliseum, Roy Rogers was grand marshal of the Sheriff's Rodeo. The Valkyries and Their Flying White Horses were showing at this rodeo in front of an audience of 102,000. Arlene remembers, "We were in the Grand Entry of the rodeo and did our square dance with Roy Rogers calling the dance. Donna jumped the five horses. Sydney and I had a three-horse Roman Race. There were a lot of Marines in the audience. As I rode by styling [waving at the audience], the Marines were whistling and waving. I won the race."

Ruth M. Davis:
A Gal's Gotta Do What a Gal's Gotta Do

When you walk into Ruth's house in Prineville, Oregon, you are immediately surrounded by a very warm, Western atmosphere. Oil paintings of horses, painted by Ruth, hang on the walls. The furniture is upholstered in a cowboy theme. A beautifully tooled Western saddle on a stand is a focal point. Tole-style lamps with Indians and cowboys, also painted by Ruth, are on every table. Photographs of Ruth when she was a trick rider vie for space among the paintings.

"You can see that I am a real horsewoman," she points out.

Hanging in her kitchen is a hand towel embroidered with Ruth's motto: "A Gal's Gotta Do What a Gal's Gotta Do." "That about sums it up for me," she laughs.

Like most trick riders, Ruth is small, standing about five feet tall in her boots. She is still slight, has a ready smile, and loves to laugh and talk about her life as a trick rider.

Ruth grew up in the Willamette Valley, just west of Salem, Oregon. Her father ran 167 acres in filberts, dairy cattle, and hay and was the barber in the nearby small town of Alsea.

Her life with horses started very early. Only she didn't ride them, she drove them. "After

Ruth Davis makes the Side Layout look easy.
Ruth M. Davis

September 1952, Ruth Davis exhibits her style! Note that, even upside down, her fingers are styled in the approved manner.

Ruth M. Davis

The Hippodrome Stand a la Ruth M. Davis!

Ruth M. Davis

Dad got sick, he would sit on the porch of the house and direct me driving the two-horse team: Dick, a gray, and Bob, a Bay, and later, Babe. I just loved that Babe. I did the discing, the harrowing, and the mowing; I was eleven years old at the time."

A trip to the Corvallis Fair pointed the way for Ruth. "I saw a trick rider and was in awe of what she did. I was already standing up on the horses, which Dad never knew about. I would go down the road, standing on Babe's back, wearing white tennis shoes. The horse just had a rope through her mouth. You know—Indian style. I must have had pretty good balance."

The plucky girl was approached by a woman in town who had pintos. She offered to sell Ruth a gelding named Governor for $75—a fortune at the time—but through hard work, Ruth managed to swing it. A partnership between girl and horse was born.

A move to Eugene, Oregon, brought Ruth her next piece of good luck. "I overheard a woman say she had a trick-riding saddle for sale. I can't imagine how I paid for that, either, but I did. I was pretty excited. Mom wasn't."

One day while she was going down the road on her horse, standing up of course, a man stopped the young Ruth. "He said, 'I'll do a deal with you. You go to church on Sundays with my wife and me, and I'll let you ride in my fields.'"

Wild Women and Tricky Ladies

With no formal training, Ruth started doing tricks on Governor. But first she had to train the horse to gallop in a straight line. "Blinkers were my key thing," she explains. "That kept him going straight ahead. I had to train the horse and me, all at the same time."

Ruth began by throwing herself around on Governor's back so that he would get used to the shifting of her weight. Eventually she was doing the Hippodrome, the Fender Drag, the Russian Drag, the One Foot Stand, and the Split to the Side, a move of her own invention. "I remembered how the woman did all the tricks at the fair. I just had pictures in my mind of the tricks, and I learned them," she says. "Some I just made up."

She started performing all over the state of Oregon. "My outfits were homemade of course," she remembers. "One was maroon with pink sleeves. I added sequins to it for some flash. Another outfit was gold with light-green pants and green pom-poms down the outsides of the legs." Ruth also was very arena savvy. "I always did the trick for the stands. I was always presented to them when I went by."

Ruth performed in arenas at Corvallis, the Philometh Frolic, Eugene, Yachats, and Newport. "I was paid, oh, maybe $50 or $75. That seemed like a lot of money to me."

Ruth was voted the Rodeo Queen for the Corvallis Rodeo in 1956. "I was out baling hay when they came and told me," she remembers. "I got a white hat, brand new. They didn't do the crowns and tiaras back then. I didn't know how to shape the hat, but a fella helped me and it turned out all right."

Ruth Davis performs her trademark Split to the Side with a smile on her face.
Ruth M. Davis

Ruth married when she was twenty-one and put her trick-riding saddle away. Babies followed. But you can't keep a cowgirl down. "I did take up barrel racing after a bit," she says.

She and her husband ranched sheep and cattle, raised Thoroughbred horses for racing, and moved around Oregon, eventually settling in Redmond in 1967.

"I've been around," Ruth says. "But the horses and trick riding were the best memories of all."

Madonna Eskew Pumphrey: A True Rodeo "Queen"

If there is royalty in rodeo, then Madonna Eskew Pumphrey wears the crown. Her family tree consists of the greats on both sides, male and female. As she puts it, "I sure couldn't have been a pastry chef!"

Her grandfather on her father's side was Col. Jim Eskew, who formed his own Wild West show in 1918. In 1930 he also started staging small rodeos, and by 1933 Colonel Eskew was staging the JE Rodeo. He is credited with making the eastern United States rodeo conscious in rodeo's early days. He used such Western stars and characters as Gene Autry, Roy Rogers and Dale Evans, the Sons of the Pioneers, the Cisco Kid and Pancho, William Boyd (Hopalong Cassidy), Lash LaRue, and Andy Devine to entertain the appreciative rodeo crowds.

The Eskew family consisted of his wife, Dolly, and two sons, Jim Jr. and Tom Mix Eskew (named for the colonel's good friend and early Western movie star). Jim Jr. trick roped, and both boys were

A young Madonna Eskew does a One-Foot Stand.
Madonna Eskew Pumphrey

When it came to trick
roping, Madonna Eskew
was a natural.
Madonna Eskew Pumphrey

Madonna Eskew with her world-famous father, Jim Eskew Jr.
Madonna Eskew Pumphrey

a great pickup team, but they also worked as arena directors and managers.

Jim "Junior" Eskew was known as "the greatest trick and fancy roper in the world." He did tricks with his rope that no one else could do.

Junior married Mary Louise Randolph, the daughter of rodeo greats Floyd and Florence Hughes Randolph. They in turn had one daughter, Madonna, born in 1941.

"When I was very little, my dad put me up on his old gelding, Star," Madonna said. "I was barely able to balance, but boy, I learned to ride. I loved it from the beginning."

The plucky little girl began performing at age five as a trick rider, taught by her grandmother Florence on her old trick-riding paint horse, Boy, who had a perfect map of the United States on one side. By age nine her father was teaching her rope spinning with his soft Maguey rope cut down to her size. "But he didn't cut it down too much," she adds. "The trick roping just came naturally."

Madonna's memories of her grandmother Florence Hughes Randolph are vivid. "Her best friend was Tad Lucas," she said. "Those two were cowgirls, all right, but they were also ladies. They would go about in fur coats and beautiful hats. They loved dressing up. It was at Tad Lucas's house that my father met my mother."

Traveling with the rodeo and Colonel Jim was a great adventure. She says, "I just got sick when fall came around and I had to go home to Oklahoma to go to school." One of the most exciting things was dressing up like a pioneer with her grandmother Dolly. "We had to act scared when the Indians came galloping in. I'd grab the dog and hide under the wagon! Various heroes like Hopalong Cassidy or Cisco and Pancho would come riding in and save us."

We wore sneakers— rubber-soled tennis shoes— which were safer and easier for jumping on and off horses.
—Vera McGinnis

In addition to performing her tricks on horseback and spinning her ropes, this all-around cowgirl hazed for her father when he competed in Rodeo Cowboys Association rodeos as a bulldogger or steer wrestler. By her twenties, Madonna was working for several stock contractors as a timer, and she carried the American flag in the Grand Entry.

On October 19, 2003, Madonna was presented with the Tad Lucas Memorial Award when she was inducted into the Rodeo Hall of Fame in Oklahoma City. The award is presented to the woman who best epitomizes Tad Lucas's love of the West and her zeal for life.

Elaine Kramer: To Ride a White Horse

In 1954 a movie called *To Ride a White Horse* featuring young women Roman riding and jumping was shown at movie theaters around the country. In the small town of Prairie du Chien, Wisconsin, a young girl named Elaine Kramer was hooked by what she saw. She saw the movie several times and noticed that it had been filmed at the White Horse Ranch in Naper, Nebraska. Elaine wrote a letter to the owners of the ranch, asking if she could come for a visit. Cal and Ruth Thompson wrote her back, inviting her to the ranch for the summer.

The Tad Lucas Award

Tad Lucas, a woman of courage, was known as "Rodeo's First Lady." No one, man or woman, rode rough stock or performed more fearlessly than Tad Lucas. She was best known for her skill as a trick rider, often performing innovative and dangerous stunts.

The Tad Lucas Award is awarded to women who have exhibited the same sort of extraordinary characteristics while upholding and promoting our great Western heritage.

Jan Mendoza

They taught Elaine to Roman ride by hooking two already trained horses together and instructing her to "go ride across that hill over there." Elaine was already an accomplished rider, but this was totally new to her. When she returned, still on top of the horses, her legs gave out from exhaustion.

Elaine Kramer, an honoree in the Cowgirl Hall of Fame, went on to achieve fame as a Roman rider. Her specialty was driving a six-horse team—four horses in front of her while she stood on two at the back.

Grandstand Caramel Corn

Just the thing to take to the rodeo while watching trick riders and ropers.
By Cowgirl Marjorie Rogers, Cowgirl Goods

6 quarts of popped corn
2 cups brown sugar
½ cup light Karo syrup
Salt to taste
2 sticks butter
½ teaspoon baking soda
1 teaspoon vanilla
Optional: 1 cup chopped pecans or peanuts

In a medium saucepan, bring the brown sugar, syrup, salt, and butter to a boil, stirring to prevent burning. Add the baking soda and vanilla—it will bubble!

Pour the syrup over the popped corn (and the nuts if you like your caramel corn "nutty"). Stir as well as you can to coat the corn. (It will be "stiff.")

Transfer this to a large, greased baking sheet. Spread it out as much as you can (it really is a gooey mess but worth the effort!) and bake at 250°F for 1 hour. (You have to move it around a bit while baking for even toasting.)

Take out of the oven and allow to cool.

Many of you have asked, "How many kernels does it take to make 6 quarts?" I found if I used my favorite soup/stew pot, covered the bottom with oil, and used ¾–1 cup of kernels, that makes about the right amount—I like mine to be well covered with the gooey stuff.

{ 4 }

TRICK RIDING TODAY:
GALLOPING INTO THE TWENTY-FIRST CENTURY

Trick riding and trick roping are as popular today as when the first wild woman shot past an amazed audience up on top of her horse, flat out and waving or spinning impossible loops that even seasoned cowhands would admire.

The wild women of today still go by at speed, and the audience is still just as amazed and enthusiastic over their display of daring and skill. No longer wearing bloomers or split skirts or the hand-sewn outfits of the middle years, today these athletic women are wearing bright tight spandex. The saddles remain the same, the horses are still the flashy paints and pintos, and the tricks are, if anything, more dangerous and heart stopping. And somewhere in the cheering crowd, a little girl is watching and dreaming and planning on growing up and doing exactly the same thing.

The trick riders of today have not forgotten their heritage and those who came before, the groundbreakers and the risk takers. Some of them are not hanging up their trick-riding saddles either. They are teaching the art to eager women who also want to stand tall on their horses.

Jan Mendoza: Doing and Teaching the Tricks

There is a small ranch in northern California, and on that ranch is an arena. Inside that arena on almost any given day, Jan Mendoza is reassuring, cajoling, and teaching nervous new prospective trick riders how to stand up on a stationary horse. The goal is to get them to stand up on a moving horse, but Jan recognizes that you have to start at the beginning. "Lean forward," Jan says to a woman teetering upright, arms waving wildly. "I know it feels all wrong, but when you are galloping—and you will be galloping—that is where the balance is."

Jan knows this from experience. She is a professional trick rider, performing at fairs, rodeos, and special events all over the West. What is it like to stand up, to go upside down, to be dragged sideways—and all the while remembering to smile and look as if it is effortless? Jan describes it like this:

Jan and her trick horse, Ima, before a performance.
Jan Mendoza

> As I let go of the reins, my horse running on her own at mach speed around the perimeter of the arena, I throw my leg over the very high saddle horn. I'm sideways now, and every part of my brain is telling me this is WRONG! I have to commit now, the crowd is watching and waiting. OK, it's now or never. I now throw my loose leg up in the air and fling my body upside down. The only thing holding me in is the strap that's around one ankle that's hooked to the saddle.
>
> It hurts! All of my muscles ache from the pounding I'm taking. My hands are dragging the dirt, the ground rushing a few inches past my face at twenty miles per hour, and I have a great big "look at me" smile on my face. As I flop like a rag doll, the crowd goes wild. I fling myself back onto the saddle, not without effort but making it look effortless, and wave to the audience.
>
> "That was the Suicide Drag, folks," the announcer yells over the loudspeaker. Another round of cheers from the rodeo audience reverberates as I set up for my next trick, my body still hurting from the last one. The adrenaline is running over me now, and the high from performing overcomes any pain I'm feeling.

Jan Mendoza is standing tall! Jan Mendoza

Jan started trick riding relatively late in life, in her early forties. "I'm an 'old lady' in this sport," she says. "Most trick riders are pretty much retired at the age of thirty-five because of injury or they decide to marry and to start families. They then teach their kids to keep the family tradition alive." Jan rode for several years in a rodeo drill team in northern California called the Painted Ladies Rodeo Performers. "I traveled with eleven other women to rodeos where we did fast precision maneuvers on running horses. We didn't do tricks, just rode our horses fast, weaving in and around each other with timed precision to music. We performed at big rodeos and rode in the Tournament of Roses Parade in Pasadena. As drill teams were becoming a dime a dozen, we decided we needed something a little different in our show. We thought it would be a thrill to ride standing up on our horses during our performance."

A group of the riders took lessons from the Riata Ranch Cowboy Girls, a trick-riding group that has been around for fifty-plus years, to learn the Hippodrome Stand. "I didn't get it right away," Jan admits, "but I came home and practiced the trick until I couldn't walk. I was finally able to master this trick on a running horse." Jan had caught trick-riding fever, and she began looking for a teacher, not an easy task.

"The Riata girls were always on the road performing and unavailable most of the

The Suicide Drag is one of trick riding's most dangerous stunts.

Jan Mendoza

time," she explains. "Finally I was lucky enough to find Rex Rossi. In his eighties when I found him, Rex was a stunt double for Roy Rogers, Clint Eastwood, Beau Bridges, and a host of other movie stars for sixty years. Rex, who wasn't physically able to show me the tricks, told me what to do and I did it. Over and over and over."

Jan studied every picture she could find of trick riders of the old days as well as the limited photos she could find of present-day trick riders on the Internet. She would show Rex a photo, and he would teach her the trick.

"After learning a dozen or so tricks, I decided to give up on the drill team and try my hand as a trick rider in rodeos. The Radical Riders Trick Team was born with young trick riders that I trained myself."

Rex passed away in 2006 at the age of eighty-seven. This inspired Jan to produce a documentary on trick riding with some basic instruction. *Trick and Fancy Riding, Past Present and Future,* released February 2008 and dedicated to the memory of Rex Rossi, is the only video about trick riding and has been sold worldwide.

"It is my hope that trick and fancy riding makes a comeback," she says. "I hope more young people discover this extreme and exciting sport and it becomes a mainstream competitive sport in the near future.

"Standing tall on a galloping horse in front of a crowd and making it look effortless is the most amazing feeling in the world!"

Standing tall on a galloping horse in front of a crowd and making it look effortless is the most amazing feeling in the world.

—Jan Mendoza

Mary Rivers: Always an Overachiever

Mary Rivers can't remember a time when she wasn't nuts about horses. Even as a little girl, she decorated her room not in frills and flounces but as a horse stall. "I even cut the door in two, like a Dutch door like they have in stables," she laughs. The windows were covered in scenes of fields—what she imagined a horse would look out on. Bits and odd pieces of tack hung on the walls.

When she was seven, she wanted riding lessons. Her father told her, "You know, there is a reason they call it the Sport of Kings. If you want to ride, you will have to work for it."

And work she did. "I mowed lawns, baby-sat, shoveled snow in the winter, and even paid my older brother the gas money to take me out to the stable for my weekly lesson."

Mary started by learning the discipline of riding hunters and jumpers. "I've always been good at being in the right place at the right time," she says. When a clinic taught by renowned rider Gordon Wright was being offered, she worked extra hard to be able to ride one of the school horses in the clinic. At the end of the clinic, Wright presented Mary with an autographed book, saying, "I'd like to present this book to the hardest working kid in the clinic."

Mary continued to learn all she could, still working several jobs to support her passion. Don Anderson came to town with his Texas White Horse Ranch Troupe and stabled his Lipizzaner horses nearby. Mary, always on the lookout for a job, brushed the horses. She was offered a job for the summer, traveling with the troupe as assistant barn manager. She rode the famous horses every day but was not allowed to ride them in the show because "there were no girls in the Spanish Riding School." But eventually Mary was doing a capriole in the show, riding sidesaddle.

A move to winter headquarters in Florida opened up another learning opportunity for Mary. Dorothy Herbert, a sidesaddle rider who was famous as a daredevil rider with the circus, noticed Mary and her talents. Dorothy's string of Liberty Ponies had gotten loose, and they were running all over the arena. "Hey, kid," Dorothy called out

Mary Rivers takes a
bow, Roman-riding
style!
Mary Rivers

to Mary. "Come here. Help me with these ponies and I'll teach you to ride sidesaddle."

Mary laughs, "I thought I knew how to ride sidesaddle, but with Dorothy I quickly learned that I didn't know how to ride sidesaddle at all!"

Mary has always had an insatiable desire to learn. If it had to do with horses, she was on it like a fly on flypaper. When she saw a Roman rider, "Boy, that sparked an interest," she says. She was thrown up onto a Roman team, and she was off. "Sure you've never done this before?" she was asked. "There was no holding me back then," Mary says. "I've always been an overachiever. It never occurred to me that I couldn't do anything with hard work and lots of practice."

Her adventures continued with a stint with the Shrine Circus and Gene Holter's Movieland Animal Show, then working as a trainer for high-diving mules. "Monkeys rode the mules, not me," Mary says. "I really didn't like those monkeys!"

One time, at the Stardust in Las Vegas, Mary was working the mules and monkeys in the parking lot before the show. "It was wet and raining," she recalls. "I was told to have a carrot for the mule as a reward and a banana for the monkey," she says. "I was also to have a towel for the monkey,

Mary Rivers jumping—sidesaddle—over fire.
Jackie Robbins/Pony City.com

whose name was Zsa Zsa, because she would be cold and wet. Well, the mule ate the carrot all right, but that monkey just slapped the banana out of my hand, unhooked her chain from the harness, and took off. I'm dressed in spandex and spangles, wearing a big Western hat, and I am running after this monkey with a banana in my hand. I can't imagine what people driving by thought." She thinks for a minute and then says, "Boy, I really hate monkeys."

Mary Rivers continues to Roman ride. Here she is, training a young team.

Mary Rivers

Mary learned to trick ride along the way, often doing a set at rodeos for day money, but Roman riding is still her first love.

It would be safe to say that anything involving a horse still holds her complete attention. With more than forty years' experience as a trainer, clinician, and performer Mary has become a trainer of both horses and people at her Dark Horse Aside/ Wild West Entertainment in Ocala, Florida. She breeds and trains Friesian horses as well as trains horses and people for performance work.

"They call me the 'Dream Maker' because I can make it happen for them," she says. "I put my heart and soul into every person I work with, and I hope they take a little bit of me away with them."

Erin Mullis: The Kamikaze Kowgirl

When Jan Mendoza was asked whom she would pick as today's rising new star in trick riding, her answer was instantaneous. "As far as upcoming trick riders, in my opinion it has to be Erin Mullis. She got her PRCA [Professional Rodeo Cowboys Association] card a few summers ago and has been really working hard making a name for herself. She does all the 'men tricks' that women just don't do today. She spent a week at my house giving ME lessons!

"There are some working trick riders out there that I know are good, but Erin just blows me away with her ability. She's doing the tricks the cowgirls in the old days did."

Erin was quick to respond with her story.

"I was the typical little girl who lived in the city and always wanted horses. Born and raised in Fort Worth, Texas, I was always fascinated by horses and farm animals alike. My parents did what they could at the time and bought me lots of toy grand champion horses to settle my longings for a real horse, but they were not real to me."

In 2001, when Erin was sixteen years old, her family moved to Keller, Texas, just outside Fort Worth. The place had a few acres on it, along with a small one-stall barn—more like a shack. This was her opportunity to get a horse.

"Newcomers to the horse industry can make some pretty bad decisions on horse buying and training," Erin notes, "and I was no exception. I found a horse trader near Burleson, Texas, and sorted through the dozens of horses for sale. I finally settled on a 'twelve-year-old bay,' which turned out to be an eighteen-year-old bay that we

For Erin Mullis, practice makes perfect.

Erin Mullis

named Rio. The journey began there. Rio wouldn't stay tied; he'd set back. I didn't know how to ride well, and we didn't know how to feed him properly."

A gentleman at Erin's high school named Mr. Brown believed she would be good at high school rodeo and helped her with the basics. "I started training for steer chasing, goat tying, and breakaway roping at NHSRA (National High School Rodeo Association). I ate the dirt many times just trying to learn how to properly ride my horse at these rodeos. Long story short, I taught myself how to ride and became fairly talented at goat tying and roping and got a full scholarship to Weatherford College to college rodeo."

The competition was hard and the money poor, so at the age of nineteen, after a year of rodeoing, Erin decided to move on to other things. She purchased a black-and-white paint to rope on and just went to open rodeos to play around. One day she was working as a flag carrier at the Stockyards Championship Rodeo in Fort Worth. A group of girls known as the Weatherford Cowgirl Chicks were there performing a drill and trick-riding routine. "The founder said that he thought I would be good at performing and invited me to join their team," she recalls. "I thanked him but put it on the back burner for a few months. When I came across the number again, I gave them a call."

Erin started practice and quickly fell in love with the team. She made good progress, and they added her to their trick-riding team. That is when she met world-renowned performers J. W. Stoker and Demetra. "This was my big break. I learned so much so fast, due to the great support network. I traveled around the country performing countless hours and became very skilled in trick riding. Television shows did many interviews and videos on the team and myself."

The Weatherford Cowgirl Chicks are listed as a nonprofit organization and thus didn't pay any of their riders. As a college girl working part-time, studying, and working on her hobbies, time became scarce; so did the money. Erin left the team.

"Some people said I would go nowhere without the Cowgirl Chicks," she recalls. "Of course this just fueled my desire to succeed. I pushed to get my trick-riding to take off, but I had to start from scratch. I lost my horse, my trick-riding saddle, and my friends. I decided to order the best-of-the-best saddle, which was a Monroe Veach brand trick-riding saddle. It would take over a year to come in, so I practiced as hard as I could in a twenty-year-old roping saddle on my black-and-white paint, Cherokee."

It was a slow process, but she slowly gathered up costumes, tack, and eventually a partner named Roni Robbins. Roni and Erin performed at amateur shows for two years as the Kamikaze Kowgirls. "She decided that it wasn't what she was looking for," Erin says. "I wanted to go pro, and she didn't want to travel far. That is when I decided to get my PRCA card and become the Kamikaze Kowgirl."

She received her PRCA card in March 2008. "Pro rodeo qualifies me for bigger and better rodeos," she explains, "which ultimately means more profit for a specialty act. I have been working my way toward the top. It is very difficult starting a business on your own, but if you can stick it out through the ups and downs, there can be many rewards for your hard work and effort. People will also respect you more for your work."

Erin has earned an associate degree from Weatherford College as well as a BS in Animal Production from Tarleton State University. But her first passion is practicing her moves on Cherokee and her tricolor paint mare, Glory.

> *It's the way you ride the trail that counts.*
> —Dale Evans

Where does this drive come from? Who inspired her? Erin says, "One of my inspirations of course is J. W. Stoker, because at seventy-nine years old he still performs and works as hard as any twenty-year-old. An accomplished performer in trick riding and roping, he has worked with so many trick riders. To hear him say that I 'can perform with the best of them' reminded me that I *can* do it!

"Of course Jan Mendoza. I met her when I was at my lowest moment, and she saw right through it and believed in me. She has supported me 100 percent and is the person I go to for a good pick-me-up when I'm down.

"I'm inspired by hardworking, humble people; when I come across people like that, it only makes me want to work harder."

Erin adds that old-time trick riders influence her more than others because she believes trick riding has gotten slack on the difficulty of the tricks. Since there are no more trick riding competitions, there is no need to do the difficult tricks. The crowd doesn't know the difference.

"You might as well do simple, easy tricks for the crowd than hard ones," she says, "but that's not my style. Those old-time trick riders risked their life for money, points, and entertainment—and they enjoyed it. I try to do a lot of groundwork and combination tricks, since that isn't seen much from women." Erin also prefers the attire of the past. "Most trick riders today wear dance costumes, very tight spandex with a Broadway appeal. It is very eye catching, but I personally like attire that matches the Western heritage. Loose clothing is dangerous, so a balance between spandex and fringe is my personal favorite, along with a good cowboy hat!"

Erin believes that trick riding is making a comeback. "I do see it more," she says, "but I think the purpose of specialty acts and trick riders is dying. We are here to entertain and please the crowd. Rodeo committees need to remember that rodeos are a family entertainment event, not completely a sport. To increase their profit, they need increased attendance. To do that they need to use specialty acts for public relations as well as big attractions for their events. Many have lost sight of this and thus lost sight of the need to keep specialty acts around.

Upside down, Erin performs with the best of them.

Erin Mullis

"It's very hard to support yourself solely as a trick rider," she admits, "but to experience the magical combination of athletic, death-defying stunts and the theatrical dance on horseback is priceless."

What does the future hold for Erin? "I plan on fulfilling my passion by getting to the bigger and better rodeos, such as the NFR (National Finals Rodeo). I am going to follow my dream of traveling the world as a professional trick and fancy rider."

Anisa, one of the talented team trick riders for Riata Ranch International, smiles as she performs the difficult Stroud Layout.

Riata Ranch: "America's Ridin' and Ropin' Royalty of the West"

Located in Exeter in California's Central Valley and nestled in the foothills of Sierra Nevada Mountains, Riata Ranch International was created in 1957 as a unique riding school for young people combining horsemanship and character development—a concept that was well ahead of its time. The program provides an opportunity to learn about our Western heritage while gaining valuable life lessons. An interesting and fun atmosphere is created while maintaining discipline and direction for an effective learning environment. The instruction is designed so that each student gains a positive set of values to guide them through the rest of their lives.

Riata Ranch International is under the direction of Jennifer Welch Nicholson, who has been associated with Riata Ranch for thirty years. She started as a young student and then became one of the four original trick-riding performers in the late 1970s. An international team leader in the 1980s through the 1990s, she has been on the administrative staff for the past ten years.

Jennifer took some time from teaching the girls to explain the philosophy behind this unique riding school. "Our vision is to prepare young people for the world's challenges in a manner that ensures their success and contributes to the happiness of everyone who is fortunate enough to meet them," she explains. "The training will benefit the whole person, body and soul, through a balance of intellectual, physi-

You earn your reputation in the arena, but you earn your respect in the barn.

—Jennifer Welch Nicholson,
Director and Cowboy Girl, Riata Ranch International

Here comes Brandi, one of Riata Ranch International's team, skimming the ground in a Full Fender.

Riata Ranch International

cal, artistic, and moral lessons. The ranch's enduring principles will become so internalized that each rider will forever measure his or her choices against the Riata Ranch philosophy."

Jennifer has entertained audiences all over the world as a Riata Ranch Cowboy Girl. She has honed her skills as a professional trick rider and trick roper and has been trained by some of the greats in the business, such as Montie Montana, J. W. Stoker, Jimmy Medeiros, Gene McLaughlin, and Vince Bruce.

Mentor and late founder of Riata Ranch, Tom Maier, taught Jennifer the founding principles and skills she uses today to teach Trick-Riding Horsemanship and Trick Ropemanship for the arena and stage. "It's about achieving greatness and striving for excellence in all areas of your life," she says.

Besides the clinics and classes she teaches at Riata Ranch, Jennifer can be hired as a motivational speaker for schools or companies. Her credits include music videos, stunt work, documentaries, professional rodeos, horse shows, clinics, and international and corporate events.

To see a performance of these skilled riders is breathtaking. Their sense of style is apparent as they spin their ropes and throw fenders at a gallop. Their pride in their polished performance and the collaboration between horse and rider and the other members of the Riata Ranch truly make them "America's Ridin' and Ropin' Royalty of the West."

Tillie, Bertha, Mabel, Fox, Prairie Rose, and all the other pioneers of fancy riding and roping would be proud.

Wild Women and Tricky Ladies

Glossary of Trick-Riding Terms

Cartwheel: a move where the rider slips to the side of the horse and turns all the way around before getting back into the saddle.

Crupper handles: two leather handles on the back of the cantle of the saddle used for the Russian, or Cossack, Drag.

Layout: to hang horizontally from the side of the horse. Leonard Stroud invented this move, called the Stroud Layout.

Maguey: a natural-fiber sixty-foot rope from Mexico. No hondas are tied on these ropes because of the many popular styles used in Maguey trick roping. As your roping skills evolve, so does your roping style. The Mexican style is slow and very graceful and uses the heavy Maguey rope.

Pitching: when the horse starts to buck.

Sell it: to do your utmost to get the trick done.

Set: a combination of tricks, or stunts.

Sold it: made a gesture at the end of a trick indicating that the audience can applaud, like throwing both arms up into the air.

Strapping: to outfit your saddle with the necessary straps on the rigging.

Strap work: to use the straps for various tricks.

Station: the area where the horse is trained to go to and then stop.

Styling: keeping your cool as you perform by pointing your toes while upside down, remembering to smile at all times, and waving to the crowd as you gallop by.

Throwing fenders: to do multiple trick moves around the saddle.

Where Cowgirls Go to Shop the Web

Sometimes a computer can be a cowgirl's best friend. I'd like to share some of my favorite places to find authentic cowgirl gear, as well as some sites that will take you into the wide-open spaces or the arena.

American Cowgirl

www.americancowgirl.com/blog

This is a site with purpose. Jamie Williams is putting together a film dedicated to cowgirls. Her photography is wonderful, and reading the postings from other cowgirls is a treat. This site is a must-see.

Anji Gallanos

http://anjigallanos.blogspot.com/2009/04/thinking-cowgirl.html

This is the site with the FABULOUS Cowgirl Rules pendants (I am getting #3) and cowboy and cowgirl earrings. Anji Gallanos is a wonderful jewelry artist. I also enjoy reading her blog.

Buckaroo Bobbins

www.fringecowgirl.com

To achieve that old-time cowgirl look (cowboys too), visit this Web site for patterns and ready-made clothing in the style of the Old West.

Cowgirl Chocolates

(888) 882-4098

www.cowgirlchocolates.com

No cowgirl can resist chocolate, and when it's COWGIRL chocolate, it's a winner! Try the truffles for a little bit of Texas in Heaven.

COWGIRLS ARE FOREVER

HANDMADE IN USA!

Roberta Maschal

Cowgirl Goods

www.cowgirlgoods.typepad.com

Marjorie Rogers makes aprons from vintage Western fabrics, embellished with old lace, buttons, and appliqué. She is developing some over-the-shoulder bags called "Saddle Bags" with the cowgirl-theme material. She also sells a great herbal healing balm in a cute little tin plus much more. Her blog is one that I follow.

Cowgirl Resale

www.cowgirlresale.com

Kate Aspen can help you look like a rodeo queen for pennies on the dollar. Gently used cowgirl clothing, boots and bags, and knockout turquoise.

Cry Baby Ranch

www.crybabyranch.com

This is the place to find the top, the skirt, the boots, the bag, the hat, the accessories—this is the place to get that cowgirl look!

Heart of a Cowgirl

http://heartofacowgirl.blogspot.com

I ordered a leather cuff with a Lone Star concho and turquoise buttons from Bridget Berthiaume, and I love it. She makes quite a bit of cowgirl jewelry at great prices. The music on her site will knock you out as well.

Jan Mendoza

www.rodeotrickrider.com

Want to learn how to stand up on a galloping horse? Visit this site and order Jan Mendoza's video. Or just watch it and dream, like I did. The photographs and postings are terrific. You will find listings of events for trick riders here as well as pictures and information on the wonderful world of trick riders from all over the United States. The Web site is unique, just like Jan. Give a howdy-shout to Jan and tell her Jill sent you.

Pendleton Cowgirl Company

www.zazzle.com/cowgirlcafeonline
This is where you will find some of the old-time cowgirls of rodeo on cards, calendars, T-shirts, mugs, and more.

Riata Ranch International

www.rrcowboygirls.com
Got a hankering for bright lights, hard work, and thunderous applause? Visit the official site for the Riata Ranch Cowboy Girls—and wear your bling!

Veach Saddlery Co., Inc.

1011 East 23rd St.
Trenton, MO 64683
(660) 359-3592
www.veachsaddlery.com
E-mail: veachsad@grm.net
Can't stand it? Just have to stand up on a galloping horse? You had better buy one of these saddles first. Trust me. Tell Peggy Veach Robinson that Jill sent you!

Rodeos and Fairs Where Trick Riding Can Be Seen

Rodeo is a tradition with deep roots. From the early days of cowpunchers just showing off to one another, rodeo has become a major sport in the United States and Canada. Trick riders and ropers are often a featured attraction at modern-day rodeos and have been a part of the tradition since the beginning. Trick riders performing at these rodeos must be PRCA (Professional Rodeo Cowboys Association) card members. This membership is hard to get—you must audition and pay substantial fees.

Grab yer hat, put on yer boots, and prepare to be amazed by thrills, chills, and spills! Here are a few of the Rodeos not to be missed:

United States
California Rodeo Salinas: One Hundred Years of Tradition
Salinas, California
Located in the midcoast area of California (think Monterey), Salinas has been home to the California Rodeo Salinas since 1911. Held in mid-July, it is the largest and most popular rodeo in California and a major stop on the professional rodeo circuit (PRCA). The Salinas rodeo (pronounced the Spanish way: *ro-DAY-o*) began in 1911 as a Wild West show on the grounds of the old racetrack.

You can view the dates, the attractions, and all the fun as well as purchase tickets online at www.carodeo.com/events-at-the-california-rodeo-salinas/tickets.

Cheyenne Frontier Days: The Daddy of 'em All
Cheyenne, Wyoming
Held annually since 1897 in the "real West" town of Cheyenne, Wyoming, this rough-

and-tough rodeo claims to be one of the largest outdoor rodeo and Western celebrations in the world. The event, which occurs over ten days around the last full week in July, draws an estimated 300,000 people to the area every year. For more information, visit www.cfdrodeo.com.

Pendleton Round-Up: "Let 'er Buck"

Pendleton, Oregon

A hundred-year-old (in 2010) Western tradition, the Pendleton Round-Up is one of America's classic rodeos. In addition to top rodeo riders, it features participating Indian tribes from the Pacific Northwest in the historic *Happy Canyon* outdoor pageant each evening. The parade features only horses and horse-drawn vehicles.

Held the end of September, the event is popular with the cowboys, cowgirls, and spectators alike. The Riata Ranch Cowboy Girls have become a favorite attraction.

For more information contact the Pendleton Round-Up Assn., Box 609, Pendleton, OR 97801; (800) 457-6336; www.pendletonroundup.com.

National Finals Rodeo: The Super Bowl of Rodeo

Las Vegas, Nevada

The NFR, the final rodeo event of the PRCA season, is held the first full week of December. World championship titles are awarded to the individuals who earn the most money in their event. Not to be missed is Cowboy Christmas, held concurrently with the NFR. Here is where you can get your cowgirl on! Visit this Web site (which will get you in the mood, I promise!) for further information: www.nfrexperience.com.

—————

Here is the link to the complete list of PRCA rodeos: http://prorodeo.com/calendar.aspx. Note that there are several hundred from which to choose.

Non-PRCA Events

Trick riders also perform at many nonprofessional or semipro rodeos outside the realm of the PRCA. You don't need a membership to ride at these rodeos, and some of them are just as big as the PRCA events! They might not be as prestigious, but they pay just the same, and the audiences are just as enthusiastic.

County fairs all over the country sometimes incorporate a rodeo during fair time, and stock contractors sometimes hire trick riders to perform. The California State Fair has trick riders almost every year. Check with your state or local chamber of commerce for information and dates.

Canada
The Calgary Stampede: "The Greatest Outdoor Show on Earth"

Calgary, Alberta

All the great trick riders and ropers have performed at this ten-day event since its beginnings. The Calgary Stampede was inaugurated in 1912 by Guy Weadick, an American trick roper who was married to trick rider and roper Florence La Due. Weadick wanted to put on a world-class rodeo event and Wild West show that would attract the best cowboys and cowgirls from across the continent.

The first Calgary Stampede, which drew more than 100,000 spectators, was the richest rodeo competition in North America with prize money totaling $20,000, and it remains one of the premier rodeo events to this day. The Stampede is one of Canada's largest annual events, and it's the world's largest outdoor rodeo. It features an internationally recognized rodeo competition, a midway, stage shows, concerts, agricultural competitions, chuck wagon races (these will take your breath away!), First Nations exhibitions, and pancake breakfasts around the city, among other attractions.

For more information check out http://cs.calgarystampede.com.

Visit www.rodeocanada.com/rodeo_schedule.html for more information on Pro Rodeo Canada events.

⎯⋯⎯

Other Events
Equine Expos

Equine expos are springing up all over the United States. Usually two or three days long, they feature clinics, demonstrations, and trade shows and usually have some sort of nightly entertainment in the main arena. Trick riders such as the Riata Ranch Cowboy Girls and the All American Cowgirl Chicks frequently entertain at these events.

Google "horse expo" and you will see the extensive list of upcoming events nationwide. Trick riders are looking at these nonrodeo events as places to perform.

Dolly Parton's Dixie Stampede

The Dixie Stampede hires trick riders as part of their big dinner show surrounding an arena. They have locations in Branson, Missouri; Myrtle Beach, South Carolina; and Pigeon Forge, Tennessee.

For more information visit www.dixiestampede.

Cavalia

Cavalia is a big-top tent horse extravaganza featuring trick riders and horses at liberty, which means they are not being ridden. It is quite a spectacle! David Carradine's daughter Kansas currently performs as a trick rider/trick roper with this show. She has been trick riding all her life. Formerly with the Riata Ranch Cowboy Girls, she now rides solo.

Visit www.cavalia.net for more information.

⎯⋯⎯

Watch the newspapers for fund-raisers and corporate events. Trick riding and roping has become a very popular entertainment.

Suggested Further Reading

Crandall, Judy. *Cowgirls: Early Images & Collectibles*. Atglen, PA: Schiffer Publishing Ltd., 1994 & 2005.

Enss, Chris. *Buffalo Gals: Women of Buffalo Bill's Wild West Show*. Guilford, CT: Globe Pequot Press/Two Dot, 2006.

Flood, Elizabeth Clair, and William Manns. *Cowgirls: Women of the Wild West*. Santa Fe, NM: Zion International Publishing, 2000.

McGinnis, Vera. *Rodeo Road: My Life as a Pioneer Cowgirl*. New York: Hastings House Publishers, 1974.

Riley, Glenda, and Richard W. Etulain. *Wild Women of the Old West*. Golden, CO: Fulcrum Publishing, 2003.

Rupp, Virgil. *Let 'er Buck! A History of the Pendleton Round-Up*. Pendleton, OR: Master Printers, 1985.

Sorensen, Lorin. *Old Time Rodeo: The Way It Was*. Santa Rosa, CA: Silverado Publishing Co., 2008.

Wade, Bob. *Bob Wade's Cowgirls*. Salt Lake City: Gibbs Smith, 1995.

Index

About the Author

Jill Charlotte Stanford lives and writes in Sisters, Oregon. She is the author of *The Cowgirl's Cookbook* (TwoDot/Globe Pequot Press) as well as several other cookbooks and *Going It Alone*, published in 2008. Visit her Web site (www.jillcharlotte.com) to see them all or visit her on Facebook.

Country Reflections; www.facebook.com/CountryReflectionsPhotography

Adora Hitchcox gives sage advice: "It does not matter how you get on a horse. It is the direction you wish to go that is important."
Adora Hitchcox